ENVIRONMENTAL EDUCATION - I

(FYBAMMC : SEMESTER - I) AS PER NEP 2020 - MUMBAI UNIVERSITY

ASHISH SHEKHAR

Made with ❤ on the Notion Press Platform
www.notionpress.com

Contents

Preface

The National Education Policy (NEP) 2020 emphasizes a holistic and multidisciplinary approach to education, with a strong focus on environmental literacy. This book has been meticulously crafted in alignment with this progressive vision for students embarking on their first semester of Environmental Education under the Open Elective (OE) category at Mumbai University, catering to BAMMC, BMS, BA, BAF, BBI, B.Com, and other courses. Our primary objective is to equip students with a profound understanding and appreciation of the environment, fostering a generation that is both knowledgeable and proactive in addressing environmental challenges.

This book delves into key environmental concepts and principles, laying a solid foundation for students to comprehend the intricate and interdependent nature of our environment. From the basic principles of ecology to the complex dynamics of climate change, each chapter is designed to build a comprehensive understanding of the environmental issues that are shaping our world today.

A significant portion of this book is dedicated to the exploration of ecosystems and biodiversity. By examining various ecosystems, from terrestrial to aquatic, and understanding the vital role biodiversity plays in maintaining the balance of nature, students will gain insights into the delicate equilibrium that sustains life on Earth. Through this, we aim to instil a sense of responsibility and urgency in preserving these natural systems.

Moreover, this book underscores the importance of responsible action and sustainable practices. By integrating theoretical knowledge with practical examples and case studies, we encourage students to translate their learning into meaningful actions that contribute to environmental conservation and sustainability. The emphasis on responsible action is designed to inspire students to become active participants in the global movement to save our planet.

The significance of environmental education cannot be overstated in today's context. With increasing environmental degradation and climate crises, the younger generation must be well-informed and proactive. This book serves as a crucial tool in this educational journey, providing students with the knowledge and motivation needed to make a positive impact on the environment.

This book is not just an academic resource; it is a call to action. By gaining a deep understanding of environmental issues and the principles governing them, students will be better prepared to contribute to a sustainable future. We hope that this book will inspire a sense of environmental stewardship and a commitment to preserving the natural world for generations to come.

Syllabus

- <u>**As Per NEP 2020**</u>
- <u>**UG First Year Programme (Semester I) - Mumbai University**</u>
- <u>**Course Details:**</u>

1. **Course Title:** Environment Education-I
2. **Course Type:** Open Elective (OE)
3. **Course Code:** Item No. -5.32 (N) Sem I (19b)
4. **Credits:** 2 Credits (1 Credit = 15 hours of theory in a semester)
5. **Hours Allotted:** 30 Hours
6. **Marks Allotted:** 50 Marks
7. **From the Academic Year:** 2024-25

- <u>**Course Description:**</u>

Environmental education represents a powerful tool for inspiring curiosity, critical thinking, and action in addressing the complex environmental challenges facing our world today. This course goes beyond traditional classroom learning; it encompasses a holistic approach that integrates knowledge, values, skills, and actions aimed at nurturing environmental literacy and fostering a deeper connection to the natural world. This course endeavours to equip educators, policymakers, activists, and community leaders with the knowledge, tools, and strategies necessary to inspire positive change and cultivate a culture of sustainability.

- **<u>Course Objectives:</u>**

The course aims to equip participants with the knowledge, skills, and motivation to become effective environmental stewards contributing to the creation of a more sustainable and resilient future for all.

1. To enhance participants' understanding of key environmental concepts, principles, and issues, fostering a foundation of environmental literacy.
2. To promote awareness and adoption of sustainable practices among participants, empowering them to take environmentally responsible actions.
3. To cultivate values through environmental education.

- **<u>Course Outcomes:</u>**

After studying the course, the students will be able to:

1. Explain key environmental concepts, principles, and issues, fostering a foundation of environmental literacy.
2. Adopt sustainable practices to take environmentally responsible actions.
3. 3. Demonstrate respect for nature and a sense of environmental responsibility.

- **<u>MODULE I: INTRODUCTION TO ENVIRONMENT EDUCATION</u>**
- **<u>Lectures: 15</u>**

1. Defining environmental education and its significance.
2. Key environmental concepts, principles, and environmental issues.

3. Responsible action to save the environment.

- **MODULE II: FOUNDATIONS OF ENVIRONMENTAL LITERACY**
- **Lectures: 15**

1. Key concepts in environmental science and environmental literacy.
2. Understanding ecosystems and biodiversity.
3. Active citizenship, acts, and policy initiatives for the environment.

- **Internal Continuous Assessment:**

1. Class Test / Assignment: 10 Marks
2. Presentation: 05 Marks
3. Classroom Participation: 05 Marks

- **Semester End Examination: 60%**
- **Format of Question Paper:**

1. Essay Type: 1 out of 2 (Module 1) - 10 Marks
2. Essay Type. 1 out of 2 (Module 2) - 10 Marks
3. Short Notes: 2 out of 4 (Module 1 & 2) - 10 Marks

Environmental Education Objectives

Environmental education aims to cultivate a deep understanding and proactive engagement with environmental issues among individuals and communities. One of its primary objectives is to **enhance environmental awareness**. This involves increasing individuals' knowledge about various environmental issues, such as climate change, pollution, and resource depletion. By providing comprehensive information on natural systems and human impacts, environmental education helps people understand the complexities of these issues and their implications for both local and global environments.

Another crucial objective is to **develop critical thinking and problem-solving skills**. Environmental education encourages individuals to analyze and evaluate environmental problems critically. It involves examining environmental data, assessing the effectiveness of various policies, and exploring sustainable solutions. This approach equips learners with the ability to make informed decisions and propose practical solutions to environmental challenges.

Fostering environmental stewardship and responsibility is also a key goal. Environmental education aims to instil a sense of personal and collective responsibility for the environment. By promoting values such as respect for nature and ethical behavior, it encourages individuals to engage in conservation efforts and adopt practices that protect and improve the environment. This sense of responsibility is essential for motivating long-term commitment to environmental sustainability.

Promoting sustainable practices and lifestyles is another important objective. Environmental education provides individuals with practical knowledge and tools to adopt environmentally-friendly behaviors in their daily lives. This includes reducing waste, conserving energy and water, and supporting sustainable consumption. By integrating these practices into everyday routines, individuals contribute to a broader culture of sustainability.

In addition, environmental education supports **community engagement and action.** It aims to involve individuals and communities in local and global environmental projects and initiatives. By facilitating community-based projects, advocacy efforts, and collaborative actions, environmental education helps address pressing environmental issues and fosters a sense of collective responsibility.

The integration of environmental education across disciplines is also a significant goal. It seeks to ensure that environmental concepts and issues are embedded within various subject areas and educational levels. This interdisciplinary approach provides a holistic understanding of environmental topics and their relevance to different fields of study.

Encouraging inquiry and experiential learning is another key objective. Environmental education promotes hands-on learning experiences and inquiry-based approaches, such as field trips and interactive activities. These methods connect theoretical knowledge with real-world applications, enhancing learners' engagement and understanding of environmental issues.

Developing skills for **environmental advocacy** is also crucial. Environmental education prepares individuals to effectively advocate for environmental policies and practices. By providing training in communication, leadership, and advocacy strategies, it empowers individuals to support environmental causes and influence decision-makers.

Furthermore, environmental education promotes **intergenerational and global perspectives.** It highlights the interconnectedness of environmental issues across generations and regions, emphasizing the impact of environmental decisions on future generations. This global perspective encourages learners to consider the broader implications of their actions and supports collaborative efforts to address worldwide environmental challenges.

Finally, preparing individuals for **future environmental challenges** is an essential objective. Environmental education equips learners with the knowledge and skills necessary to tackle emerging and evolving environmental issues. By focusing on adaptive strategies, innovation, and resilience, it ensures that individuals are well-prepared to address future environmental conditions and challenges.

Lastly, the objectives of environmental education are designed to foster a well-informed, responsible, and proactive population capable of addressing environmental issues effectively. By focusing on awareness, critical thinking, stewardship, and practical action, environmental education empowers individuals to contribute to a sustainable future and promotes a culture of environmental responsibility.

CHAPTER I

Environment education and its significance

Environmental education is the process of learning about the natural world and how human activities impact the environment. It aims to raise awareness and understanding of environmental issues, encouraging individuals to develop the knowledge, skills, and attitudes necessary to make informed decisions and take responsible actions to protect and sustain the environment.

The significance of environmental education lies in its ability to foster a sense of connection and responsibility towards the natural world. As people become more aware of environmental issues such as climate change, pollution, deforestation, and biodiversity loss, they are more likely to engage in behaviours that contribute to environmental conservation and sustainability. By understanding the intricate relationships between humans and the environment, individuals can appreciate the importance of conserving natural resources and protecting ecosystems for future generations.

Environmental education also plays a crucial role in promoting sustainable development. It equips individuals with the knowledge and skills to address environmental challenges and develop innovative solutions. This is particularly important in a world where environmental degradation and resource depletion threaten human well-being and economic stability. By fostering critical thinking and problem-solving skills, environmental education empowers people to make decisions that balance environmental, social, and economic considerations, leading to more sustainable lifestyles and communities.

Furthermore, environmental education enhances the quality of life by promoting healthier and more sustainable living practices. For example, learning about the benefits of reducing waste, conserving energy, and using renewable resources can lead to more environmentally friendly behaviours that improve air and water quality, reduce greenhouse gas emissions, and preserve natural habitats. This, in turn, contributes to better health outcomes and a higher quality of life for individuals and communities.

In addition to individual benefits, environmental education has broader societal impacts. It encourages civic engagement and community participation in environmental protection initiatives. By fostering a sense of environmental stewardship, it motivates people to advocate for policies and practices that promote environmental sustainability. This collective action is essential for addressing large-scale environmental issues that require coordinated efforts at local, national, and global levels.

Environmental education is vital for creating a more informed and environmentally responsible society. It promotes awareness, understanding, and action on environmental issues, leading to more sustainable and healthier lifestyles. By empowering individuals and communities to make environmentally conscious decisions, environmental education plays a critical role in protecting and preserving the natural world for present and future generations.

CHAPTER II

Key concepts, principles & issues

Understanding key environmental concepts and definitions is essential for informed decision-making, effective communication, and problem-solving. It helps individuals and policymakers make choices that consider ecological impacts, fosters clear discussions among stakeholders and supports the development of strategies to address environmental issues. Additionally, it raises awareness about the importance of conservation and aids in crafting effective policies and regulations. This knowledge is crucial for promoting sustainability and tackling complex environmental challenges. Understanding and applying environmental principles can help us make more sustainable choices and create a healthier, more resilient planet for future generations.

Key environmental concepts

- **Ecosystems** - An ecosystem is a community of living organisms (plants, animals, and microbes) interacting with their physical environment (such as air, water, and soil). These interactions create a web of relationships that support life. For example, in a forest ecosystem, trees provide oxygen, homes for animals, and help retain soil, while animals like birds and insects help pollinate plants and control pests. Each component, whether living or non-living, plays a crucial role in maintaining the balance and health of the ecosystem.

- **Biodiversity** - Biodiversity refers to the variety of life on Earth, including the different species of plants, animals, bacteria, and fungi. High biodiversity means a large number of different species, which contributes to ecosystem stability and resilience. Each species has a role in the ecosystem, such as pollination, decomposition, or being part of the food chain. When biodiversity is high, ecosystems are more adaptable to changes and can recover more easily from disruptions like diseases or natural disasters.

- **Climate Change** - Climate change is the long-term alteration of temperature and typical weather patterns in a place. It is primarily caused by human activities, such as burning fossil fuels (like coal, oil, and natural gas) and deforestation. These activities increase the concentration of greenhouse gases in the atmosphere, which trap heat and cause the Earth's temperature to rise. The impacts of climate change include more frequent and severe weather events, rising sea levels, and disruptions to natural ecosystems and human societies.

- **Sustainability** - Sustainability is the practice of meeting our present needs without compromising the ability of future generations to meet their own needs. It involves using resources in a way that maintains their availability for the long term. This includes managing natural resources like water, soil, and forests responsibly, reducing waste and pollution, and transitioning to renewable energy sources. Sustainable practices aim to balance environmental health, economic prosperity, and social well-being.

- **Renewable Energy** - Renewable energy comes from sources that are naturally replenished on a human timescale, such as sunlight, wind, rain, tides, waves, and geothermal heat. Unlike fossil fuels, which are finite and contribute to pollution and climate change, renewable energy sources are cleaner and more sustainable. Solar panels and wind turbines are common examples of technologies that harness renewable energy. Transitioning to renewable energy helps reduce greenhouse gas emissions and reliance on non-renewable resources.

- **Pollution** - Pollution is the introduction of harmful substances or products into the environment, which can affect air, water, and land. Common pollutants include chemicals, plastics, heavy metals, and waste products. Pollution can have serious health impacts on humans and animals, damage ecosystems, and contribute to climate change. Efforts to reduce pollution include using cleaner technologies, reducing waste, recycling, and enforcing environmental regulations.

- **Conservation** - Conservation is the protection and management of natural resources to prevent exploitation, degradation, and destruction. It involves preserving natural habitats, protecting endangered species, and maintaining biodiversity. Conservation efforts can include establishing protected areas like national parks, restoring damaged ecosystems, and promoting sustainable land use practices. The goal of conservation is to ensure that natural resources are available for future generations and that ecosystems remain healthy and functional.

Environmental principles

- **Sustainability** - Sustainability is about meeting our present needs without compromising the ability of future generations to meet their own needs. It involves using natural resources responsibly and efficiently, ensuring that ecosystems remain healthy and productive over time. This principle encourages us to think long-term and consider the environmental impact of our actions on the planet and its inhabitants.

- **Biodiversity** - Biodiversity refers to the variety of life on Earth, including different species of plants, animals, and microorganisms, as well as the ecosystems they form. High biodiversity ensures natural sustainability for all life forms. It provides us with resources such as food, medicine, and clean water, and helps maintain ecosystem balance. Protecting biodiversity is crucial for the resilience and health of our environment.

- **Interconnectedness** - This principle highlights the interconnected nature of all living and non-living components of the Earth. Everything in the environment is linked, and changes in one part can affect others. For instance, pollution in a river can impact the fish population, which in turn affects birds that feed on fish. Understanding these connections helps us make more informed decisions to protect and preserve the environment.

- **Precautionary Principle** - The precautionary principle states that if an action or policy has the potential to cause harm to the environment or human health, and there is a lack of scientific consensus on the matter, the burden of proof falls on those advocating for the action. This principle encourages caution and preventive measures, promoting actions that avoid harm even when scientific knowledge is incomplete or uncertain.

- **Polluter Pays Principle** - This principle asserts that those who produce pollution should bear the costs of managing it to prevent damage to human health or the environment. It aims to internalize environmental costs, ensuring that the price of goods and services reflects their environmental impact. By holding polluters accountable, this principle promotes cleaner production methods and encourages businesses to reduce their environmental footprint.
- **Environmental Justice** - Environmental justice emphasizes that all people, regardless of race, nationality, or income, should have equal access to a clean and healthy environment. It addresses the disproportionate impact of environmental hazards on marginalized and disadvantaged communities. This principle seeks to ensure fair treatment and meaningful involvement of all individuals in environmental decision-making processes.
- **Conservation** - Conservation involves the careful management and protection of natural resources to prevent their depletion. It focuses on preserving ecosystems, wildlife, and natural habitats, ensuring that they remain intact for future generations. Conservation efforts can include creating protected areas, sustainable forestry practices, and measures to reduce human impact on the environment.
- **Ecosystem Services** - Ecosystem services are the benefits that humans derive from ecosystems, such as clean air and water, pollination of crops, and climate regulation. Recognizing the value of these services is essential for sustainable development. By preserving and enhancing ecosystem services, we ensure that natural systems continue to support human well-being

and economic stability.

Environmental issues & its cause

- **Climate Change** - Climate change is one of the most pressing environmental issues today. It is caused by the increase in greenhouse gases, such as carbon dioxide, methane, and nitrous oxide, in the atmosphere. These gases trap heat from the sun, causing the Earth's temperature to rise. This leads to a range of impacts including more frequent and severe weather events like hurricanes, droughts, and heatwaves, melting polar ice caps, rising sea levels, and shifts in wildlife populations and habitats. Human activities, particularly the burning of fossil fuels for energy and deforestation, are the main drivers of climate change.

Climate change is primarily driven by human activities that increase the concentration of greenhouse gases in the atmosphere. Burning fossil fuels for energy, such as coal, oil, and natural gas, releases significant amounts of carbon dioxide. Deforestation also contributes to climate change because trees that absorb carbon dioxide are removed, reducing the Earth's capacity to manage this greenhouse gas. Industrial processes, agricultural practices, and waste management further release methane and nitrous oxide, intensifying the greenhouse effect.

- **Deforestation** - Deforestation refers to the large-scale removal of forests, a major environmental concern. Forests play a crucial role in absorbing carbon dioxide, producing oxygen, and supporting biodiversity. However, forests are being cut down at an alarming rate for agriculture, logging, and urban development. This leads to habitat loss for many species, reduces biodiversity, and contributes to climate change by releasing stored carbon dioxide into the atmosphere. Protecting and restoring forests is essential for maintaining ecological balance and mitigating climate change.

Deforestation happens due to several human activities. The need for agricultural land to grow crops and raise livestock leads to clearing forests. Logging for timber and paper products also contributes to deforestation. Urban expansion and infrastructure development require land, often leading to the destruction of forests. Illegal logging and lack of enforcement of environmental regulations exacerbate the problem. Economic factors, such as the demand for palm oil, soy, and beef, drive large-scale deforestation, especially in tropical regions.

- **Pollution** - Pollution is the introduction of harmful substances into the environment, and it comes in various forms: air, water, and soil pollution. Air pollution, caused by emissions from vehicles, industries, and burning of fossil fuels, leads to respiratory diseases and environmental degradation. Water pollution, resulting from industrial waste, agricultural runoff, and sewage discharge, contaminates drinking water sources and harms aquatic life. Soil pollution, due to pesticides, heavy metals, and waste disposal, affects crop production and human health. Reducing pollution requires stricter regulations, better waste management, and the adoption of cleaner technologies.

Pollution is largely a result of industrialization and modern lifestyles. Air pollution stems from the burning of fossil fuels in vehicles, power plants, and factories, releasing pollutants like sulfur dioxide, nitrogen oxides, and particulate matter. Water pollution occurs when industrial discharge, agricultural runoff (containing fertilizers and pesticides), and untreated sewage enter water bodies. Soil pollution is caused by the use of chemical fertilizers, pesticides, and the improper disposal of industrial and household waste. Inadequate waste management and lack of regulations contribute to widespread pollution.

- **Loss of Biodiversity** - Biodiversity, the variety of life on Earth, is crucial for ecosystem stability and resilience. However, human activities such as deforestation, pollution, climate change, and overfishing are causing significant loss of biodiversity. Many species are becoming endangered or extinct, which disrupts ecosystems and diminishes natural resources like food, medicine, and clean water. Protecting biodiversity involves creating and enforcing wildlife conservation laws, establishing protected areas, and promoting sustainable practices that minimize environmental impact.

Biodiversity loss is driven by habitat destruction, pollution, climate change, over-exploitation of resources, and invasive species. Deforestation, urban development, and agriculture destroy natural habitats. Pollution from chemicals, plastics, and other pollutants harms wildlife.

Climate change alters habitats and food sources, making survival difficult for many species. Overfishing, hunting, and poaching reduce animal populations. Invasive species introduced by human activities outcompete native species for resources, further reducing biodiversity.

- **Plastic Waste** - Plastic waste is a growing environmental problem, particularly in oceans. Plastics are durable and take hundreds of years to decompose, leading to accumulation in the environment. Marine animals often mistake plastic debris for food, which can be fatal. Microplastics, tiny plastic particles, are also entering the food chain, posing health risks to humans and wildlife. Reducing plastic waste requires measures such as banning single-use plastics, improving waste management systems, and encouraging recycling and the use of alternative materials.

Plastic waste is a result of the widespread use of plastic products, which are cheap, versatile, and durable. The convenience of single-use plastics, such as packaging, bottles, and bags, leads to large amounts of waste. Inadequate waste management systems and low recycling rates contribute to plastic pollution. Improper disposal of plastics, littering, and lack of public awareness exacerbate the problem. The long lifespan of plastics means they persist in the environment for hundreds of years, accumulating in landfills and oceans.

- **Water Scarcity** - Water scarcity affects millions of people worldwide and is exacerbated by climate change, pollution, and over-extraction of water resources. Freshwater is essential for drinking, agriculture, and sanitation, but it is becoming increasingly scarce in many regions. Sustainable water management practices, such as efficient irrigation, rainwater harvesting, and wastewater treatment, are critical for ensuring a reliable supply of clean water. International cooperation and investment in water infrastructure are also necessary to address this issue.

Water scarcity is driven by several factors, including population growth, increased demand for water, and climate change. As the global population grows, so does the demand for water for drinking, agriculture, and industry. Climate change leads to altered precipitation patterns, causing droughts in some regions and floods in others, disrupting water availability. Pollution of freshwater sources reduces the amount of clean water available. Over-extraction of groundwater for agriculture and industrial use depletes aquifers faster than they can be replenished. In many places, inefficient water use and poor management practices exacerbate the problem.

CHAPTER III

Action to save environment

Taking action to save the environment is necessary because the health of our planet directly affects the well-being of all living organisms, including humans. Environmental degradation, such as deforestation, pollution, and climate change, leads to the loss of biodiversity, disrupts ecosystems, and poses significant threats to human health. For example, air and water pollution can cause respiratory diseases and contaminate drinking water sources, while climate change increases the frequency of extreme weather events, resulting in devastating impacts on communities and economies. By taking proactive steps to protect and restore the environment, we can ensure a healthier, more stable planet for current and future generations.

The need for immediate action is underscored by the accelerating pace of environmental decline. Scientific evidence shows that we are approaching critical tipping points, beyond which the damage to ecosystems may become irreversible. This urgency demands swift and decisive measures to reduce greenhouse gas emissions, conserve natural habitats, and transition to sustainable practices. Moreover, addressing environmental issues now can provide economic benefits, such as job creation in green industries and reduced costs associated with climate-related disasters. By acting promptly, we can mitigate the worst impacts of environmental degradation, safeguard natural resources, and build a resilient, sustainable future.

Reduce, Reuse, Recycle

- **Reduce** - Reducing waste involves making conscious decisions to minimize the amount of disposable items we use. For instance, bringing a reusable shopping bag to the store instead of using plastic bags can greatly reduce plastic waste. Similarly, using a reusable water bottle instead of buying bottled water helps cut down on plastic waste. Opting for products with minimal packaging, or choosing bulk items, also helps in reducing the amount of waste generated. Additionally, reducing energy consumption by turning off lights when not in use, using energy-efficient bulbs, and unplugging electronics can decrease your carbon footprint.

- **Reuse** - Reusing items extends their life cycle and reduces the need for new products. For example, old glass jars can be reused as storage containers for pantry items or leftovers, instead of buying new plastic containers. Clothes that are no longer in fashion or fit can be donated or repurposed into cleaning rags or even upcycled into new clothing items. Reusing shopping bags, using rechargeable batteries, and repurposing old furniture are other ways to practice reuse. Buying second-hand items from thrift stores or online marketplaces also supports the reuse principle and reduces waste.

- **Recycle** - Recycling involves processing used materials into new products, which conserves natural resources and reduces landfill waste. Common recyclables include paper, cardboard, glass, aluminium cans, and certain plastics. It's important to follow local recycling guidelines to ensure materials are properly sorted and processed. For example, rinsing out food containers before recycling can prevent contamination and ensure they can be recycled efficiently. Electronics, batteries, and certain hazardous materials often have specific recycling programs, which prevent harmful substances from entering the environment.

Conserve Energy and Water

- **Energy Conservation** - Energy conservation can be achieved through simple everyday actions. For example, setting your thermostat a few degrees lower in the winter and higher in the summer can reduce heating and cooling costs. Using energy-efficient appliances, such as LED light bulbs and Energy Star-rated devices, reduces energy consumption. Turning off lights, computers, and other electronics when they are not in use prevents wasted energy. Additionally, using public transportation, biking, or carpooling reduces fossil fuel consumption and lowers greenhouse gas emissions.
- **Water Conservation** - Water conservation involves using water more efficiently and preventing waste. Fixing leaky faucets and pipes can save significant amounts of water. Installing low-flow showerheads and faucets, as well as dual-flush toilets, reduces water usage. Taking shorter showers and only running dishwashers and washing machines with full loads are simple ways to conserve water. Collecting rainwater for garden use and choosing drought-resistant plants for landscaping are other effective water-saving strategies.

Support Sustainable Practices

- **Conscious Consumerism** - Supporting sustainable practices involves making informed choices about the products and services you use. For instance, buying products made from recycled or sustainable materials reduces the demand for new resources. Opting for fair-trade and organic products supports ethical and environmentally friendly production methods. Supporting local farmers and businesses reduces the environmental impact of transportation and stimulates the local economy. By choosing companies with strong environmental policies, you encourage more businesses to adopt green practices.
- **Reducing Carbon Footprint** - Reducing your carbon footprint can be achieved by altering your lifestyle choices. For example, reducing meat consumption and incorporating more plant-based meals into your diet can lower greenhouse gas emissions associated with livestock farming. Choosing to walk or bike for short trips instead of driving reduces fossil fuel use. Travelling by train instead of flying for long-distance trips can significantly reduce your carbon footprint. Additionally, supporting renewable energy sources, like solar or wind power, contributes to the reduction of fossil fuel reliance.

Community Involvement

- **Participating in Community Clean-up Events** - Community clean-up events are organized efforts where volunteers gather to clean up local parks, beaches, streets, and other public areas. These events help to remove litter and pollutants, improving the aesthetics and health of these spaces. For example, the Ocean Conservancy's International Coastal Cleanup mobilizes millions of volunteers each year to remove trash from beaches and waterways around the world. Such clean-ups help to protect wildlife from ingesting or getting entangled in debris, reduce water pollution, and foster community pride and environmental stewardship.
- **Tree Planting Initiatives** - Planting trees is a highly effective way to combat climate change, as trees absorb carbon dioxide, provide oxygen, and improve air quality. Community tree-planting programs, like the Arbor Day Foundation's initiatives, encourage individuals and groups to plant trees in urban and rural areas. Trees also provide shade, reduce urban heat islands, support biodiversity, and can even improve mental health by creating greener, more pleasant environments. Local governments and organizations often offer tree-planting events and provide free or discounted trees to residents.
- **Supporting Local Conservation Projects** - Local conservation projects aim to protect and restore natural habitats, preserve biodiversity, and maintain ecosystem services. Examples include efforts to restore wetlands, reforest degraded lands, and protect local wildlife. In the U.S., programs like the Conservation Reserve Program (CRP) pay farmers to convert environmentally sensitive agricultural land into habitats that can support wildlife and reduce soil erosion. Joining or donating to local

conservation groups, volunteering for habitat restoration projects, and participating in citizen science initiatives can all support these vital efforts.

- **Environmental Education and Awareness** - Raising awareness about environmental issues and educating others is key to driving change. This can involve organizing or attending workshops, seminars, and educational programs in schools, libraries, and community centres. For instance, initiatives like Earth Day events focus on environmental education and involve activities like recycling drives, eco-friendly product fairs, and sustainability workshops. Educated communities are more likely to adopt sustainable practices and support environmental policies.

Advocating for Policy Change

- **Supporting Environmental Legislation** - Environmental legislation is critical for enforcing regulations that protect the environment. Supporting laws that address issues like pollution control, wildlife conservation, and renewable energy adoption is essential. For example, the Clean Air Act and Clean Water Act in the U.S. set standards for air and water quality, which have significantly reduced pollution levels. By contacting local representatives, signing petitions, and voting for candidates who prioritize environmental issues, individuals can influence the creation and enforcement of such laws.
- **Joining Environmental Advocacy Groups** - Environmental advocacy groups, such as the Sierra

Club, Greenpeace, and the World Wildlife Fund (WWF), work to influence public policy and promote environmental conservation. These organizations conduct research, raise awareness, and lobby for legislative changes. Joining or supporting these groups can amplify efforts to address environmental issues on a larger scale. Members can participate in campaigns, attend rallies, and contribute to advocacy efforts that push for stronger environmental protections.

- **Promoting Renewable Energy Policies** - Transitioning to renewable energy sources like wind, solar, and hydropower is crucial for reducing greenhouse gas emissions and combating climate change. Advocating for policies that support the development and adoption of renewable energy can drive significant environmental benefits. For instance, Germany's Energiewende policy has successfully increased the country's renewable energy share, reducing reliance on fossil fuels. Supporting incentives for renewable energy projects, tax credits for clean energy investments, and research funding for new technologies can help accelerate this transition.

- **Engaging in Local Government** - Active participation in local government can directly influence environmental policy at the community level. Attending city council meetings, joining local planning committees, and participating in public consultations on environmental issues can give individuals a voice in local decision-making processes. For example, residents can advocate for green infrastructure projects, such as bike lanes, public transportation improvements, and urban green spaces, which can enhance sustainability and quality of life in their communities.

Everyday Habits for Environmental Conservation

- **Mindful Consumption** - High-Quality and Durable Products: Investing in high-quality, durable items reduces the need for frequent replacements, thereby decreasing waste and resource consumption. For example, buying a well-made pair of shoes that lasts several years is more sustainable than purchasing cheaper shoes that wear out quickly and need frequent replacement.

- **Repairing and Reusing** - Repairing items instead of discarding them extends their life and reduces waste. Simple actions like sewing a torn piece of clothing, fixing a broken appliance, or refurbishing old furniture can make a big difference. For example, repairing a smartphone screen instead of buying a new phone helps reduce electronic waste.

- **Reducing Overall Consumption** - Mindful consumption involves thinking critically about your purchases and avoiding impulse buys. Asking yourself whether you really need an item, whether it will add value to your life, and considering its environmental impact can help reduce unnecessary consumption. For example, before buying a new piece of clothing, consider whether it complements your existing wardrobe, if you can find a similar item second-hand, or if you truly need it.

- **Reduce Single-Use Plastics** - Opting for reusable items instead of single-use plastics is a simple yet impactful habit. Carry a reusable water bottle, shopping bag, and coffee cup with you to avoid disposable alternatives. For example, using a stainless steel water bottle instead of buying plastic bottles can significantly cut down on plastic waste. Additionally, refusing plastic straws and utensils by carrying your own reusable set can further reduce your plastic footprint.

- **Conserve Water** - Being mindful of water usage in daily activities can greatly contribute to environmental conservation. Simple habits like turning off the tap while brushing your teeth, taking shorter showers, and fixing leaks promptly can save gallons of water. For instance, collecting rainwater to water your garden or using a broom instead of a hose to clean driveways and sidewalks are practical ways to conserve this vital resource.

Practical Examples

- **Reusable Bags and Containers:**Using reusable bags, bottles, and containers can significantly reduce the amount of single-use plastic waste. Carrying a reusable shopping bag and a stainless steel water bottle can eliminate the need for plastic bags and disposable water bottles.
- **Energy-Efficient Appliances:** Switching to energy-efficient appliances, such as LED bulbs, smart thermostats, and energy star-rated refrigerators, can reduce energy consumption and lower utility bills. For example, replacing incandescent bulbs with LED ones can save energy and last longer.

- **Eco-Friendly Transportation:** Choosing eco-friendly transportation options like biking, walking, carpooling, or using public transit reduces carbon emissions. For instance, biking to work instead of driving reduces fuel consumption and greenhouse gas emissions.
- **Minimalist Lifestyle:** Adopting a minimalist lifestyle, which focuses on owning fewer but more meaningful possessions, can lead to reduced waste and a lower environmental impact. For example, decluttering your home and donating items you no longer need promotes reuse and reduces the demand for new products.

CHAPTER IV

Global Warming

Global warming refers to the long-term increase in Earth's average surface temperature due to human activities, primarily the emission of greenhouse gases (GHGs). This phenomenon results from the accumulation of these gases, such as carbon dioxide (CO_2), methane (CH_4), and nitrous oxide (N_2O), in the atmosphere. These gases trap heat from the sun, creating a "greenhouse effect" that prevents the heat from escaping back into space. As a result, the planet's surface and lower atmosphere gradually warm up, leading to a variety of environmental and climatic changes.

The concept of global warming is closely linked to the broader phenomenon of climate change, which encompasses not only the rise in global temperatures but also the associated shifts in weather patterns, sea levels, and other climatic conditions. While natural factors like volcanic eruptions and variations in solar radiation have historically influenced Earth's climate, the current trend of rapid warming is largely driven by human activities, particularly the burning of fossil fuels, deforestation, and industrial processes. These activities have significantly increased the concentration of greenhouse gases in the atmosphere since the Industrial Revolution, accelerating the rate of global warming and its impacts on the environment, ecosystems, and human societies.

Understanding global warming is crucial because it poses significant risks to the planet's health and the well-being of all its inhabitants. The effects of global warming include more frequent and severe weather events, rising sea levels, melting polar ice, and disruptions to ecosystems and biodiversity. These changes have far-reaching consequences, affecting food security, water resources, human health, and economies worldwide. Therefore, addressing global warming through mitigation efforts, such as reducing greenhouse gas emissions and transitioning to renewable energy sources, as well as through adaptation strategies to manage its impacts, is essential for ensuring a sustainable and resilient future for the planet.

Causes of Global Warming

Greenhouse Gas Emissions - The primary driver of global warming is the increase in greenhouse gases (GHGs) in the Earth's atmosphere. Greenhouse gases trap heat from the sun, preventing it from escaping back into space, and thereby warming the planet. The most significant greenhouse gases contributing to global warming include carbon dioxide (CO_2), methane (CH_4), nitrous oxide (N_2O), and fluorinated gases.

- **Carbon Dioxide (CO_2)** is the most prevalent greenhouse gas linked to human activities. It is primarily produced by the burning of fossil fuels such as coal, oil, and natural gas for energy. When these fuels are combusted in power plants, vehicles, and industrial processes, they release large amounts of CO_2. Additionally, deforestation exacerbates the issue; trees act as carbon sinks, absorbing CO_2 from the atmosphere. When forests are cut down or burned, the stored carbon is released back into the atmosphere, increasing CO_2 levels and reducing the planet's capacity to absorb future emissions.

- **Methane (CH4)**, although less abundant than CO2, is much more effective at trapping heat. Methane is released during the production and transport of fossil fuels, as well as from livestock digestion and rice paddies. Livestock, such as cows and sheep, produce methane during digestion through a process called enteric fermentation. Additionally, decomposing organic matter in landfills emits methane. Because of its potency as a greenhouse gas, even small increases in methane concentration can significantly impact global warming.
- **Nitrous Oxide (N2O)** is another significant greenhouse gas, released from agricultural and industrial activities. In agriculture, the use of nitrogen-based fertilizers results in the emission of nitrous oxide as microorganisms in the soil convert the fertilizers into N2O. Industrial processes, including the production of chemicals and fossil fuel combustion, also contribute to nitrous oxide emissions. Despite its lower concentration compared to CO2, N2O has a substantial warming effect due to its high heat-trapping capability.
- **Fluorinated Gases** include a variety of synthetic chemicals used in industrial applications, such as refrigerants, solvents, and propellants. These gases, including hydrofluorocarbons (HFCs), perfluorocarbons (PFCs), and sulfur hexafluoride (SF6), are not naturally occurring and are released through industrial processes and the disposal of products containing them. While these gases are present in smaller quantities, they are extremely potent in trapping heat and can remain in the atmosphere for long periods, contributing to long-term warming.

Deforestation - Deforestation is a significant contributor to global warming because it decreases the number of trees that can absorb CO_2 from the atmosphere. Forests act as carbon sinks, sequestering large amounts of carbon dioxide through photosynthesis. When trees are cut down or burned, the carbon stored in their biomass is released back into the atmosphere as CO_2. Additionally, deforestation disrupts local and global water cycles, leading to reduced precipitation and further exacerbating the effects of global warming. The clearing of forests for agriculture, logging, and urban development significantly contributes to increased atmospheric CO_2 levels.

Industrial Activities - Industrial activities contribute substantially to global warming through the emission of greenhouse gases and pollutants. Manufacturing processes, particularly those involved in the production of cement, steel, and chemicals, release large amounts of CO_2 and other greenhouse gases. Industrial facilities also often emit methane and nitrous oxide, contributing further to global warming. Additionally, many industrial processes involve the use of energy derived from fossil fuels, which contributes indirectly to greenhouse gas emissions. The expansion of industrial activities and infrastructure often leads to increased fossil fuel consumption and greenhouse gas emissions, compounding the problem of global warming.

Agriculture - Agriculture plays a dual role in global warming, both through direct emissions of greenhouse gases and indirectly through changes in land use. Livestock production generates significant amounts of methane during digestion (enteric fermentation) and from manure management. The rice paddies also produce methane due to the anaerobic conditions created by flooding.

Agricultural soils emit nitrous oxide as a byproduct of fertilizer application and soil management practices. Moreover, the conversion of forests and wetlands into agricultural land releases stored carbon and reduces the land's capacity to sequester CO2. The combined effects of these agricultural practices contribute notably to global warming.

Urbanization - Urbanization contributes to global warming through increased energy consumption, higher greenhouse gas emissions, and the heat island effect. As cities expand, the demand for energy for heating, cooling, and powering buildings grows, leading to increased fossil fuel consumption and emissions. Urban areas often experience higher temperatures than surrounding rural areas due to the heat island effect, where buildings, roads, and other infrastructure absorb and re-emit heat. This localized warming further exacerbates overall global temperature increases. Additionally, the expansion of urban areas often involves deforestation and the destruction of natural habitats, which further contributes to greenhouse gas emissions and reduces the planet's natural carbon sinks.

Addressing Impacts

- **Environmental Impact** - Addressing global warming is crucial due to its profound impact on the environment. One of the most visible effects is rising sea levels, driven by the melting of ice caps and glaciers and the thermal expansion of seawater. As sea levels rise, coastal communities face increased flooding, erosion, and the loss of vital habitats. This not only threatens the homes and livelihoods of millions but also leads to the destruction of important ecosystems like mangroves and wetlands, which provide crucial services such as storm protection and carbon sequestration.

Extreme weather events are becoming more frequent and severe due to global warming. Heatwaves, hurricanes, droughts, and heavy rainfall events are intensifying, causing widespread damage to infrastructure, agriculture, and natural ecosystems. For example, more intense storms can lead to devastating flooding and property damage, while prolonged droughts can deplete water supplies and harm crops. These environmental changes disrupt ecosystems, leading to shifts in species distributions and the loss of biodiversity, which can have cascading effects on food chains and ecosystem health.

- **Human Health** - The health impacts of global warming are significant and multifaceted. Increased temperatures and more frequent heatwaves can lead to heat-related illnesses such as heat exhaustion and heatstroke, particularly affecting vulnerable populations like the elderly and those with preexisting health conditions. Higher temperatures can also exacerbate air pollution, leading to respiratory problems and cardiovascular diseases. For instance, ground-level ozone, which is more prevalent in warmer conditions, can aggravate asthma and other respiratory conditions.

Global warming also affects the spread of vector-borne diseases. Changes in temperature and precipitation patterns can expand the range of insects that carry diseases such as malaria, dengue fever, and Zika virus. As these vectors move into new regions, they expose populations that previously had no immunity to these diseases, potentially leading to outbreaks and increased public health challenges.

- **Economic Impact** - The economic implications of global warming are extensive and varied. Agriculture, a sector directly dependent on climate conditions, faces risks from changing temperatures and precipitation patterns. Altered growing seasons and increased frequency of extreme weather events can reduce crop yields, disrupt food supply chains, and drive up food prices. This can lead to economic instability, particularly in regions heavily reliant on agriculture, and exacerbate food insecurity globally.

Infrastructure is also at risk from the impacts of global warming. Rising sea levels and more intense weather events can damage roads, bridges, and buildings, leading to costly repairs and economic disruptions. For example, increased flooding can undermine transportation networks and utilities, affecting businesses and communities. The financial burden of adapting infrastructure to withstand these changes can be substantial, requiring significant investment and resources.

Energy costs are another area affected by global warming. Higher temperatures lead to increased demand for cooling, which strains energy resources and drives up costs. Conversely, extreme weather events can disrupt energy supplies and infrastructure, leading to outages and further economic impacts. Transitioning to more energy-efficient systems and renewable energy sources can help mitigate these costs and improve energy resilience.

- **Social Impact** - Global warming also has significant social implications. As climate impacts such as rising sea levels and extreme weather events intensify, they can lead to displacement and migration. Communities in vulnerable regions may be forced to relocate, leading to social and political challenges as they move to new areas. This can strain resources and infrastructure in receiving communities and lead to conflicts over land and resources.

Competition for resources such as water and arable land can also heighten social tensions. As these resources become scarcer due to the effects of global warming, conflicts may arise between different groups or nations. Ensuring equitable access to resources and implementing effective management strategies are crucial for maintaining social stability and avoiding conflicts.

- **Global Cooperation** - Addressing global warming requires coordinated international efforts and cooperation. Climate change is a global issue that transcends national borders, and its impacts are felt worldwide. International agreements, such as the Paris Agreement, aim to unite countries in their commitment to reducing greenhouse gas emissions and promoting sustainable development. By working together, nations can share knowledge, technologies, and resources to tackle climate change more effectively.

Collaboration between governments, businesses, and civil society is essential for implementing climate policies and achieving global climate goals. Public awareness and individual actions also play a vital role in driving change and supporting broader climate initiatives. By addressing global warming through collective action, we can work towards a more sustainable and resilient future for all.

Importance of Mitigation

Mitigation refers to efforts aimed at reducing or preventing the emission of greenhouse gases to limit global warming and its associated impacts. Effective mitigation is crucial for slowing the pace of climate change and avoiding the most severe consequences. One of the primary strategies for mitigation is transitioning to renewable energy sources. Fossil fuels, such as coal, oil, and natural gas, are the largest contributors to greenhouse gas emissions. By shifting to renewable energy sources like wind, solar, and hydropower, we can significantly cut down on carbon dioxide emissions. Investing in renewable energy not only reduces our reliance on fossil fuels but also supports sustainable development and creates new economic opportunities.

Another key aspect of mitigation is improving energy efficiency. Energy efficiency measures reduce the amount of energy required to perform the same tasks, which decreases overall energy consumption and emissions. For instance, upgrading to energy-efficient appliances, insulating buildings to reduce heating and cooling needs, and promoting energy-efficient transportation options can collectively lower greenhouse gas emissions. Additionally, adopting sustainable practices in agriculture, such as reducing methane emissions from livestock and implementing conservation tillage, can further contribute to emission reductions.

Afforestation and reforestation are also critical components of mitigation. Trees absorb carbon dioxide from the atmosphere, acting as natural carbon sinks. Planting trees and restoring degraded forests not only sequesters carbon but also enhances biodiversity, improves water quality, and supports local communities. By incorporating these strategies, we can address the root causes of global warming and work towards a more sustainable and resilient future.

Importance of Adaptation

Adaptation involves adjusting to the impacts of global warming to minimize damage and protect communities. As the effects of climate change become increasingly apparent, adaptation measures are essential for reducing vulnerability and building resilience. Infrastructure resilience is a key area of focus. Investing in the development and retrofitting of infrastructure to withstand extreme weather events, such as hurricanes, floods, and heatwaves, can prevent costly damage and protect lives. For example, constructing flood defences, elevating buildings in flood-prone areas, and improving drainage systems are vital adaptation strategies that help communities cope with changing conditions.

Disaster preparedness is another critical component of adaptation. Developing early warning systems, emergency response plans, and community-based disaster management programs enhances our ability to respond effectively to natural disasters. These measures can mitigate the impacts of extreme weather events, safeguard public health, and reduce economic losses. Training and educating communities about disaster preparedness and response also empower individuals to take proactive steps in safeguarding their homes and families.

Water management is increasingly important as climate change affects precipitation patterns and water availability. Implementing efficient water use practices, such as rainwater harvesting, water recycling, and improved irrigation techniques, helps ensure a reliable water supply despite changing conditions. Additionally, investing in water infrastructure, such as reservoirs and pipelines, can enhance resilience to droughts and floods.

Both mitigation and adaptation are necessary for addressing global warming comprehensively. While mitigation aims to prevent further climate change by reducing greenhouse gas emissions, adaptation focuses on managing the impacts that are already occurring or anticipated. By integrating these approaches, we can better prepare for and respond to the challenges posed by a changing climate, ultimately fostering a more sustainable and resilient world.

CHAPTER V

Acid Rain

Acid rain is a type of precipitation that contains higher-than-normal levels of sulfuric and nitric acids, making it more acidic than regular rainwater. This phenomenon occurs when pollutants like sulfur dioxide (SO_2) and nitrogen oxides (NO_x), primarily released from burning fossil fuels in power plants, vehicles, and industrial processes, react with water vapour in the atmosphere. The resulting acids are carried by wind and precipitation, falling to the ground as acid rain. This acidic precipitation can take the form of rain, snow, fog, or even dust, and it can have harmful effects on the environment, structures, and human health.

Impact on Ecosystems

One of the most significant impacts of acid rain is on aquatic ecosystems. When acid rain falls into rivers, lakes, and streams, it lowers the pH levels of the water, making it more acidic. This can be detrimental to aquatic life, particularly fish and amphibians, as it disrupts their ability to reproduce and survive. For example, in the 1970s and 1980s, many lakes in the northeastern United States and Canada became so acidic that they could no longer support fish populations, leading to significant ecological disruptions. Acid rain also leaches important nutrients from the soil, weakening trees and plants and making them more susceptible to disease, pests, and extreme weather conditions.

Effects on Human-Made Structures

Acid rain not only affects natural ecosystems but also damages human-made structures. Buildings, monuments, and bridges made of limestone, marble, and concrete are particularly vulnerable. The acids in acid rain react with the calcium compounds in these materials, causing them to dissolve and wear away over time. A notable example is the erosion of historical monuments such as the Parthenon in Greece and the Taj Mahal in India. The Taj Mahal, in particular, has suffered from acid rain, which has caused the white marble to turn yellow and develop a rough surface. This deterioration has led to extensive restoration efforts to preserve these cultural landmarks.

The Black Triangle

One of the most notorious examples of acid rain occurred in the "Black Triangle," a heavily industrialized region located at the border of Germany, Poland, and the Czech Republic. During the mid-20th century, this area experienced severe environmental degradation due to the high concentration of coal-fired power plants and factories that released large amounts of sulfur dioxide and nitrogen oxides into the air. The resulting acid rain had devastating effects on the local environment, causing widespread damage to forests, lakes, and rivers. Many lakes became so acidic that they could no longer support aquatic life, and vast areas of forests died off due to the inability of trees to absorb essential nutrients from the acidified soil.

Efforts to Reduce Acid Rain

To combat acid rain, significant efforts have been made to reduce the emissions of sulfur dioxide and nitrogen oxides. One of the most successful initiatives was the U.S. Clean Air Act Amendments of 1990, which introduced a cap-and-trade program for SO_2 emissions. This program incentivized industries to adopt cleaner technologies and reduce their emissions, leading to a significant decrease in acid rain. Additionally, international cooperation has played a key role in addressing transboundary pollution, as acid rain can affect regions far from the pollution sources. Despite these efforts, acid rain remains a concern in some parts of the world, underscoring the need for continued vigilance and global cooperation to protect the environment.

CHAPTER VI

Science & Literacy

Environmental Science

Environmental science is a field of study that explores the interactions between living organisms and their surroundings. It combines knowledge from various scientific disciplines, including biology, chemistry, geology, and ecology, to understand how natural systems work and how human activities impact the environment.

The core of environmental science involves examining natural processes, such as the water cycle, nutrient cycles, and energy flow, and studying how these processes are affected by human actions. For example, scientists look at how pollution affects air and water quality, how deforestation impacts biodiversity, and how climate change alters weather patterns and ecosystems.

By understanding these interactions, environmental scientists aim to address environmental problems and develop solutions that promote sustainability. They work on issues like reducing pollution, conserving natural resources, and protecting endangered species. Their work often involves collecting and analyzing data, conducting experiments, and using models to predict future environmental conditions.

Environmental science is an interdisciplinary field that studies the interactions between humans and the natural environment. Its key concept revolves around understanding how these interactions affect the environment and how we can address environmental issues to promote sustainability.

At its core, environmental science examines the components of the environment, which include the atmosphere, hydrosphere (water bodies), lithosphere (land), and biosphere (living organisms). It looks at how these components work together in complex systems and how human activities can disrupt these systems. For example, pollution from factories can contaminate air and water, affecting both wildlife and human health. Environmental scientists study these impacts to develop strategies for reducing or mitigating negative effects.

One fundamental principle in environmental science is the concept of sustainability. Sustainability focuses on meeting current needs without compromising the ability of future generations to meet their own needs. This involves using resources like water, energy, and minerals in ways that do not deplete them or cause irreversible damage to ecosystems. For instance, using renewable energy sources like solar or wind power instead of fossil fuels helps reduce greenhouse gas emissions and combat climate change.

Another important concept is the idea of ecological balance. Ecosystems are dynamic and complex networks of living organisms interacting with each other and their physical environment. Disruptions to one part of an ecosystem can have ripple effects throughout the system. For example, removing a predator species from a habitat can lead to an overpopulation of prey species, which can, in turn, lead to overconsumption of vegetation and loss of plant species. Environmental science seeks to understand these relationships and how human actions can either support or disrupt ecological balance.

In addition, environmental science emphasizes the importance of environmental policy and management. Governments and organizations develop policies and regulations based on scientific research to protect natural resources and promote environmental health. This includes setting standards for air and water quality, managing protected areas, and addressing issues like climate change and biodiversity loss. Effective environmental management relies on understanding the scientific principles behind these issues and applying them to make informed decisions.

Lastly, Environmental science provides a comprehensive understanding of how humans interact with the environment and offers solutions for maintaining a healthy and sustainable planet. By studying the natural world and our impact on it, environmental scientists aim to foster a balance that supports both human well-being and the health of the Earth.

Environmental Literacy

Environmental literacy refers to the knowledge and skills needed to understand and engage with environmental issues. It's about being informed about how the environment works and how our actions influence it.

Being environmentally literate means you know basic concepts about the environment, such as how ecosystems function, the importance of biodiversity, and the impacts of human activities on the planet. It also involves understanding key environmental issues like climate change, resource depletion, and pollution, and being able to make informed decisions that contribute to environmental sustainability.

Environmental literacy includes not only factual knowledge but also critical thinking skills. It involves the ability to analyze information, evaluate sources, and make reasoned decisions about environmental practices. This literacy is crucial for addressing environmental challenges, as it empowers individuals to take responsible actions, advocate for environmental policies, and contribute to community efforts aimed at protecting and improving the environment.

In essence, while environmental science provides the detailed understanding of environmental processes and issues, environmental literacy equips individuals with the tools to use that knowledge in everyday life and decision-making.

Environmental literacy refers to the understanding of the natural world and the role humans play within it. It involves knowledge of ecological principles, environmental issues, and the skills needed to make informed decisions about the environment. This concept encompasses not only awareness and knowledge but also attitudes, behaviors, and actions that contribute to environmental sustainability.

At its core, environmental literacy includes an understanding of the interconnections between human and natural systems. This means recognizing how human activities, such as agriculture, industry, and urban development, impact the environment and how these impacts can affect human health and well-being. It also involves understanding the natural processes that sustain life on Earth, such as the water cycle, energy flow, and biodiversity.

One key aspect of environmental literacy is the ability to critically evaluate environmental information. This includes distinguishing between credible and non-credible sources, understanding scientific data, and recognizing the socio-economic and political dimensions of environmental issues. Being environmentally literate means being able to participate in discussions and debates about environmental policies and practices in an informed and meaningful way.

Environmental literacy also emphasizes the importance of responsible environmental behavior. This includes taking personal and collective action to reduce environmental impact, such as conserving energy and water, reducing waste, and supporting sustainable practices. It also means advocating for policies and practices that promote environmental health and sustainability.

Lastly, environmental literacy is about being informed and proactive about environmental issues. It combines knowledge, critical thinking, and responsible behavior to foster a sustainable relationship between humans and the natural world. By cultivating environmental literacy, individuals and communities can better address the complex environmental challenges of today and work towards a more sustainable future.

CHAPTER VII

Ecosystems & Biodiversity

Understanding Ecosystems

An ecosystem is a community of living organisms interacting with their physical environment. It includes all the plants, animals, and microorganisms in a given area, along with their non-living environments such as water, soil, and air. These components are linked together through nutrient cycles and energy flows. For example, in a forest ecosystem, trees provide oxygen and habitats for animals. Animals, in turn, contribute to the nutrient cycle through their waste and, eventually, their decomposition.

Ecosystems can vary greatly in size and type, from small ponds to vast deserts and dense forests. Each ecosystem has its own unique combination of living and non-living components that interact in complex ways. These interactions can be as simple as plants absorbing sunlight and nutrients from the soil or as complex as predator-prey relationships in a rainforest. Regardless of size or complexity, every ecosystem plays a crucial role in maintaining the balance of the natural world.

Ecosystem Services

Ecosystem services are the benefits that humans derive from ecosystems. These services are broadly categorized into four types: provisioning, regulating, supporting, and cultural services. Provisioning services include the supply of food, water, and raw materials. Regulating services involve the control of climate, disease, and water quality. Supporting services are necessary for the production of all other ecosystem services, such as nutrient cycling and soil formation. Cultural services encompass non-material benefits, such as recreation, aesthetic enjoyment, and spiritual fulfilment.

Healthy ecosystems with high biodiversity are more likely to provide these services efficiently and sustainably. For instance, wetlands with diverse plant and animal life can better filter pollutants from water, protect against floods, and provide habitat for fish and birds. The interdependence of species within ecosystems ensures that these services are maintained, highlighting the need for biodiversity conservation in maintaining human well-being.

By understanding the intricate relationships within ecosystems and the importance of biodiversity, we can better appreciate the natural world and our role in preserving it. Through informed actions and policies, we can work towards a sustainable future where both nature and humanity thrive.

Examples of Ecosystems

Forest Ecosystem

A forest ecosystem consists of trees, shrubs, herbs, and various animal species. The trees play a crucial role in absorbing carbon dioxide and releasing oxygen through photosynthesis. Leaf litter from trees decomposes and enriches the soil, supporting plant growth. Animals, such as birds, insects, and mammals, interact with the plants by pollinating flowers, dispersing seeds, and serving as prey or predators, thus maintaining the ecosystem's balance.

Coral Reef Ecosystem

Coral reefs are underwater ecosystems characterized by reef-building corals. These ecosystems are incredibly diverse, hosting numerous species of fish, crustaceans, mollusks, and marine plants. Corals form symbiotic relationships with algae, which provide them with food through photosynthesis. The structure of coral reefs provides habitat and protection for many marine species, while also protecting coastlines from erosion by dissipating wave energy.

Desert Ecosystem

Deserts are characterized by low rainfall and extreme temperatures. Despite the harsh conditions, deserts support a variety of life forms. Plants like cacti store water in their tissues, while animals such as camels and lizards have adapted to survive with minimal water. The interaction between these organisms and their environment allows for nutrient cycling and energy flow in an otherwise challenging habitat.

Understanding Biodiversity

Biodiversity refers to the variety of life in a particular ecosystem or across the entire planet. It includes all species of plants, animals, fungi, and microorganisms, as well as the genetic diversity within these species. Biodiversity is essential for ecosystem stability and resilience. It ensures that ecosystems can recover from disturbances, adapt to changes, and continue to provide essential services such as clean air and water, pollination of crops, and regulation of climate.

The richness of biodiversity can be seen in different ecosystems. For example, tropical rainforests and coral reefs are known for their high levels of biodiversity, hosting a wide range of species that interact in intricate and often interdependent ways. Conversely, ecosystems with low biodiversity, such as arctic tundras or deserts, may seem less diverse but still play vital roles in the global ecosystem.

The Importance of Biodiversity

Biodiversity is critical for the health and functioning of ecosystems. High biodiversity increases ecosystem productivity, as each species has a specific role to play in maintaining ecological balance. For instance, diverse plant species ensure soil health and stability, which in turn supports a variety of animal life. Furthermore, genetic diversity within species allows populations to adapt to changing environmental conditions, reducing the risk of extinction.

The loss of biodiversity, often due to human activities such as deforestation, pollution, and climate change, poses a significant threat to ecosystems and the services they provide. Conservation efforts are crucial to protect biodiversity and ensure the sustainability of our natural resources. By preserving habitats, reducing pollution, and promoting sustainable practices, we can help maintain the balance of ecosystems and safeguard the planet's biodiversity for future generations.

Examples of Biodiversity

Tropical Rainforest Biodiversity

Tropical rainforests are known for their extraordinary biodiversity. In these ecosystems, you'll find a vast array of plant species, including towering trees, vines, and epiphytes. Animals such as jaguars, monkeys, birds, and countless insects inhabit the forest, each playing a role in the ecosystem. The dense vegetation and complex food webs support a high level of species interactions, contributing to the overall health and resilience of the ecosystem.

Agricultural Biodiversity

Agricultural biodiversity refers to the variety of crops and livestock species used in farming. Diverse crop systems, such as those incorporating multiple species or varieties, can enhance soil health, reduce pest outbreaks, and improve resilience to climate change. For example, a farm that grows a mix of grains, legumes, and vegetables alongside livestock like chickens and cows can create a more sustainable and productive system compared to monoculture farming.

Marine Biodiversity

Marine ecosystems, such as those found in the open ocean and coastal areas, host a wide range of species. From microscopic plankton to large whales, the diversity in marine life forms is immense. Coral reefs, seagrass beds, and mangrove forests are examples of marine habitats with high biodiversity. This diversity is crucial for maintaining the health of the ocean, supporting fisheries, and providing livelihoods for millions of people.

CHAPTER VIII

Acts and Policies

Active citizenship involves individuals actively participating in the civic and political life of their communities to bring about positive change. When it comes to the environment, active citizenship is crucial because it helps drive the development and implementation of policies that protect natural resources, reduce pollution, and promote sustainability. Active citizenship is indispensable for effective environmental protection. Through advocacy, participation in policy-making, and community initiatives, citizens can drive significant environmental improvements. Acts like the Clean Air Act, international agreements like the Paris Agreement, and community-led projects demonstrate the power of collective action in safeguarding our planet for future generations. By staying informed, engaged, and proactive, individuals can contribute to a healthier, more sustainable world.

The Clean Air Act (CAA)

The Clean Air Act (CAA) is a vital federal law in the United States aimed at regulating air emissions from various sources to ensure air quality meets health and safety standards. Originally enacted in 1963, it has been significantly strengthened through amendments in 1970 and 1990, empowering the Environmental Protection Agency (EPA) to establish National Ambient Air Quality Standards (NAAQS). These standards are designed to protect public health, especially vulnerable groups, and to mitigate the environmental impacts of air pollution.

To achieve its objectives, the CAA requires states to create State Implementation Plans (SIPs) that detail how they will meet and maintain the NAAQS, subject to EPA approval. The act also imposes regulations on emissions from industrial sources, power plants, and vehicles, including limits on hazardous air pollutants and the adoption of advanced emission control technologies. Additionally, the CAA addresses broader issues like acid rain, ozone depletion, and toxic air pollutants, making it a comprehensive approach to managing air quality.

A key success of the CAA is its impact on reducing sulfur dioxide (SO_2) emissions, a major contributor to acid rain. The 1990 amendments introduced a cap-and-trade program for SO_2 emissions from power plants, which set a national cap and allowed plants to trade emissions allowances. This market-driven approach has led to significant reductions in SO_2 levels, particularly from coal-fired power plants, resulting in a marked decrease in acid rain and improved air quality.

The success of the CAA has been bolstered by active public engagement, with community groups and environmental organizations playing crucial roles in monitoring air quality and advocating for stronger standards. Despite the progress made, challenges remain, including addressing climate change-related pollutants and ensuring equitable air quality improvements for all communities. Continued public participation and vigilant enforcement are essential to maintaining and advancing the gains achieved under the Clean Air Act.

The Paris Agreement

The Paris Agreement, adopted on December 12, 2015, is a key international treaty under the United Nations Framework Convention on Climate Change (UNFCCC). Its main goal is to limit global warming to well below 2 degrees Celsius above pre-industrial levels, with efforts to keep the temperature increase to 1.5 degrees Celsius. The agreement emphasizes enhancing adaptive capacity, resilience, and reducing vulnerability to climate change, marking a departure from the Kyoto Protocol by requiring all nations to contribute to the global effort through nationally determined contributions (NDCs).

Under the Paris Agreement, countries must submit NDCs, which outline their climate actions, including targets for reducing greenhouse gas emissions and strategies for adapting to climate change. These contributions are to be updated every five years, with increasing ambition over time. The flexibility of NDCs allows countries to set goals based on their circumstances, fostering a sense of collective responsibility while accommodating varying national contexts.

Germany's approach under the Paris Agreement highlights how the treaty influences national policies. Germany aims to achieve greenhouse gas neutrality by 2045, with a Climate Action Plan that includes phasing out coal by 2038, increasing renewable energy use, and promoting electric vehicles. The country has introduced policies like the Renewable Energy Sources Act and a carbon pricing scheme to support these targets, though challenges like infrastructure investment and balancing economic growth with sustainability remain.

The Paris Agreement promotes international cooperation, with countries like Germany leading by example and inspiring others to strengthen their climate commitments. Through mechanisms such as the Green Climate Fund, developed nations provide financial assistance to developing countries, supporting global climate actions and resilience. Despite challenges, the agreement encourages continuous improvement, aiming for a more sustainable and resilient global future.

The European Green Deal

The European Green Deal, introduced by the European Commission in December 2019, is a strategic plan aimed at making Europe the first climate-neutral continent by 2050. It includes various policies designed to reduce greenhouse gas emissions, promote sustainable economic growth, and protect natural habitats, serving as the EU's roadmap for a sustainable future.

A major element of the Green Deal is the "Fit for 55" package, which aims to cut net greenhouse gas emissions by 55% by 2030, compared to 1990 levels. This involves revising the EU Emissions Trading System to cover more sectors, including maritime transport, and implementing a Carbon Border Adjustment Mechanism to prevent carbon leakage. These measures push industries to innovate and reduce their carbon emissions.

The Green Deal also emphasizes a transition to renewable energy and improved energy efficiency, targeting a 40% share of renewables in the EU's energy mix by 2030. Investments in wind, solar, and hydropower are key to this goal, along with initiatives like the "Renovation Wave," which aims to enhance energy efficiency in buildings. These efforts help reduce reliance on fossil fuels while creating jobs.

Furthermore, the Green Deal promotes a circular economy and the protection of biodiversity. The Circular Economy Action Plan focuses on reducing waste and improving product design, while the EU Biodiversity Strategy for 2030 aims to protect and restore ecosystems. The Just Transition Mechanism ensures that the transition to a green economy is fair, providing financial support to regions most affected by the shift from fossil fuels to sustainable industries.

Key Environmental Acts in India

India has enacted several important laws to protect and manage the environment. These acts address a range of environmental issues, from pollution control to biodiversity conservation. These acts collectively form the backbone of India's environmental legal framework, addressing various aspects of environmental protection and sustainable development. They reflect the country's commitment to preserving its natural resources and ensuring a healthy environment for its citizens.

The Environment (Protection) Act, 1986
The Environment (Protection) Act, 1986, is a comprehensive piece of legislation aimed at safeguarding and improving the environment. It provides a framework for the central government to coordinate the activities of various central and state authorities established under previous environmental laws. The Act empowers the government to set environmental standards, regulate industrial pollution, and establish penalties for non-compliance. Under this Act, the government has issued

several rules and notifications, such as the Hazardous Waste (Management and Handling) Rules, 1989, and the Environmental Impact Assessment Notification, 2006, which mandates environmental clearances for various projects.

The Water (Prevention and Control of Pollution) Act, 1974

The Water (Prevention and Control of Pollution) Act, 1974, was one of the earliest efforts to regulate water pollution in India. It established the Central Pollution Control Board (CPCB) and State Pollution Control Boards (SPCBs) to monitor and control water pollution by enforcing standards and taking legal action against violators. The Act aims to prevent and control water pollution by addressing the discharge of pollutants into water bodies, ensuring the quality of water for various purposes, and promoting the use of sewage treatment plants.

The Air (Prevention and Control of Pollution) Act, 1981

The Air (Prevention and Control of Pollution) Act, 1981, focuses on controlling and reducing air pollution. Similar to the Water Act, it established the CPCB and SPCBs to implement air quality standards and regulate emissions from industrial plants and vehicles. The Act empowers these boards to inspect air pollution control equipment, issue directives to industries, and initiate legal proceedings against offenders. It also provides for the establishment of air quality monitoring stations across the country.

The Forest (Conservation) Act, 1980

The Forest (Conservation) Act, 1980, aims to protect and conserve forests in India. It restricts the de-reservation of forests or the use of forest land for non-forest purposes without prior approval from the central government. The Act plays a crucial role in maintaining the ecological balance by preserving forest cover and promoting afforestation. It also seeks to ensure that any diversion of forest land for development projects, such as dams or roads, is compensated by afforestation on an equivalent area of non-forest land.

The Wildlife (Protection) Act, 1972

The Wildlife (Protection) Act, 1972, was enacted to protect and conserve wildlife in India. It provides for the creation of protected areas, such as national parks, wildlife sanctuaries, and conservation reserves, to safeguard habitats and species. The Act prohibits hunting of endangered species and regulates trade in wildlife products. It also establishes advisory boards at the central and state levels to oversee wildlife conservation efforts and enforce penalties for violations.

The National Green Tribunal Act, 2010

The National Green Tribunal (NGT) Act, 2010, established the NGT, a specialized judicial body to handle environmental disputes and enforcement of legal rights related to the environment. The NGT aims to ensure the expeditious resolution of environmental cases, thereby reducing the burden on regular courts. It has the power to order compensation for environmental damage, restore damaged ecosystems, and impose penalties for non-compliance with environmental laws.

Key Environmental Policies in India

India has implemented a range of policies and initiatives aimed at protecting the environment and promoting sustainable development.These policies address various environmental challenges, including air and water pollution, deforestation, and climate change. These policies reflect India's commitment to addressing environmental challenges and promoting sustainable development. They involve a combination of regulatory measures, economic incentives, public awareness campaigns, and community participation to achieve their objectives.

National Environment Policy (NEP) 2006

The National Environment Policy (NEP) 2006 provides a framework for environmental protection and sustainable development in India. The policy emphasizes the need for an integrated approach to environmental management, considering the interconnections between various environmental issues. It outlines several objectives, including the conservation of critical environmental resources, the integration of environmental concerns into development planning, and the enhancement of environmental governance. The NEP promotes the use of economic principles in environmental decision-making, such as the "polluter pays" principle and the use of market-based instruments.

Forest Conservation Act (FCA) 1980

The Forest Conservation Act (FCA) 1980 aims to regulate the use of forest land for non-forest purposes. It requires prior approval from the central government for any diversion of forest land for activities such as mining, industrial projects, and infrastructure development. The FCA seeks to curb deforestation and promote the conservation of forest resources. It also includes provisions for compensatory afforestation, where project developers must plant trees to compensate for the loss of forest cover.

Air (Prevention and Control of Pollution) Act 1981 and Water (Prevention and Control of Pollution) Act

1974

The Air (Prevention and Control of Pollution) Act 1981 and the Water (Prevention and Control of Pollution) Act 1974 are key legislations aimed at controlling pollution in India. The Air Act provides for the establishment of Central and State Pollution Control Boards to monitor and regulate air pollution. It sets standards for emissions from industrial plants and vehicles and mandates measures to control air pollution. Similarly, the Water Act focuses on the prevention and control of water pollution. It establishes regulatory authorities to oversee water quality and enforce pollution control measures. Both acts emphasize the importance of public participation and awareness in combating pollution.

National Action Plan on Climate Change (NAPCC) 2008

The National Action Plan on Climate Change (NAPCC) 2008 outlines India's strategy to tackle climate change through eight national missions. These missions cover various aspects of climate action, including solar energy, enhanced energy efficiency, sustainable agriculture, and water resource management. The NAPCC emphasizes the need to balance economic growth with environmental sustainability. It promotes the adoption of clean technologies, the development of renewable energy sources, and the implementation of energy-efficient practices. The NAPCC also highlights the importance of building resilience to climate impacts through measures such as improved water management and sustainable agriculture.

Swachh Bharat Abhiyan (Clean India Mission) 2014

Launched in 2014, Swachh Bharat Abhiyan is a nationwide campaign aimed at improving sanitation and cleanliness across India. The mission seeks to eliminate open defecation, improve waste management practices, and promote hygiene and sanitation awareness. It involves the construction of toilets, the establishment of solid waste management systems, and the promotion of behavior change through public awareness campaigns. Swachh Bharat Abhiyan has significantly contributed to improving sanitation infrastructure and public health in both urban and rural areas.

National Green Tribunal (NGT) Act 2010

The National Green Tribunal (NGT) Act 2010 established the NGT, a specialized judicial body responsible for expediting the resolution of environmental cases. The NGT provides a platform for individuals and organizations to seek redress for environmental grievances and ensures the enforcement of environmental laws and regulations. It has the authority to hear cases related to environmental protection, conservation of forests, and natural resource management. The NGT plays a crucial role in strengthening environmental governance and accountability in India.

Community-Led Environmental Initiatives

Beyond large-scale policies and agreements, grassroots movements and community-led initiatives play a crucial role in environmental conservation. Examples include local recycling programs, community gardens, and clean-up drives for rivers and beaches. These initiatives often start with a small group of dedicated individuals who mobilize their communities to take action. Such efforts not only improve local environments but also raise awareness about broader environmental issues and inspire others to get involved.

Case Studies

Case Study I - The Eco-Schools Program in Finland

- **Background** - Finland is renowned for its commitment to environmental sustainability, and the Eco-Schools Program is a prime example of how environmental education can be integrated into the school system. Launched in the early 2000s, the program is part of the international Eco-Schools network, which aims to encourage schools to implement eco-friendly practices and educate students about environmental issues.
- **Implementation** - In Finland, the Eco-Schools Program involves a comprehensive approach where schools commit to adopting sustainable practices across their operations. This includes initiatives like reducing energy consumption, promoting recycling, and integrating environmental topics into the curriculum. Each participating school forms an "Eco-Committee" composed of students, teachers, and sometimes parents, who work together to create and implement an Environmental Action Plan.
- **Outcomes** - The Eco-Schools Program has led to significant improvements in environmental awareness and behavior among students. Schools that participate often report a decrease in waste production and energy usage. For instance, a school in Helsinki reduced its annual energy consumption by 20% after adopting energy-saving measures. Additionally, the program has

fostered a sense of environmental responsibility among students, with many participating schools noting an increase in students' environmental activism and understanding.

- **Impact** - The success of the Eco-Schools Program in Finland has demonstrated the effectiveness of integrating environmental education into school curricula and operations. It has not only improved environmental practices within schools but also empowered students to become advocates for sustainability in their communities. The program has received recognition from various environmental organizations and continues to serve as a model for other countries aiming to promote environmental education.

• • •

Case Study II - The "Green School" Initiative in Bali, Indonesia

- **Background** - The "Green School" in Bali, Indonesia, is a pioneering example of how environmental education can be effectively implemented in an international school setting. Established in 2008, Green School is known for its commitment to sustainability and its innovative approach to environmental education. The school offers a curriculum that emphasizes hands-on learning and real-world applications of environmental principles.

- **Implementation** - Green School's approach to environmental education is deeply embedded in its philosophy and daily operations. The school operates on a 20-acre campus designed with sustainability in mind, featuring bamboo buildings, solar panels, and a natural water filtration system. The curriculum is designed to integrate environmental education into all subjects, with a strong focus on experiential learning. Students participate in projects related to organic farming, waste management, and renewable energy. The school also encourages community involvement through workshops and outreach programs.

- **Outcomes** - The Green School has achieved notable successes in both environmental stewardship and educational outcomes. Students are actively involved in maintaining the school's sustainable practices, such as managing the school's permaculture garden and participating in waste reduction programs. Academic performance has also benefited from the hands-on, project-based learning approach, with students demonstrating increased engagement and creativity in their studies. The school's environmental initiatives have also had a positive impact on the local community, with many residents adopting sustainable practices inspired by the school's example.

- **Impact** - Green School in Bali has set a new standard for how environmental education can be integrated into school life and the broader community. Its innovative approach has attracted international attention and has become a model for schools worldwide seeking to adopt sustainable practices and foster environmental awareness among students. The school's success underscores the potential for educational institutions to drive positive change in environmental practices and inspire future generations of environmentally conscious leaders.

• • •

Case Study III - The "Green Schools" Initiative in Tamil Nadu, India

- **Background** - The "Green Schools" initiative in Tamil Nadu, India, is a notable example of how environmental education can be effectively implemented in a diverse and resource-constrained setting. Launched by the Tamil Nadu Pollution Control Board (TNPCB) in collaboration with various NGOs and educational institutions, the initiative aims to integrate environmental education into school curricula and promote sustainable practices within schools.
- **Implementation** - The Green Schools initiative focuses on a holistic approach to environmental education by incorporating sustainability principles into both the curriculum and school operations. Participating schools are encouraged to establish Eco-Clubs, where students and teachers collaborate on environmental projects and

activities. The initiative provides schools with training, resources, and guidelines to help them develop and implement environmental action plans. Key components include waste management programs, water conservation efforts, and energy-saving measures. Schools also engage in activities such as tree planting, recycling drives, and awareness campaigns on local environmental issues.

- **Outcomes** - The Green Schools initiative has achieved significant success in raising environmental awareness and promoting sustainable practices among students and staff. Schools that participate in the program have reported improvements in waste management and reductions in resource consumption. For example, a school in Coimbatore implemented a waste segregation and composting program that reduced its waste by 30% and generated organic fertilizer for use in its gardens. Additionally, students have shown increased environmental consciousness and responsibility, with many initiating community projects focused on sustainability.

- **Impact** - The Green Schools initiative has had a profound impact on both the educational and environmental landscapes in Tamil Nadu. By integrating environmental education into school curricula and fostering a culture of sustainability, the initiative has empowered students to become proactive in addressing environmental challenges. The program has also demonstrated that even in resource-limited settings, it is possible to achieve significant environmental and educational outcomes through collaboration and innovative approaches. The success of the initiative has inspired other regions in India to adopt similar programs, contributing to a broader movement towards environmental education and sustainability across the country.

• • •

Case Study IV - The "Green School" Initiative in India: The Kothari International School

- **Background** - The Kothari International School in Noida, India, is a prime example of integrating environmental education into school life. Founded in 2006, the school has made environmental sustainability a cornerstone of its educational philosophy. The initiative began as part of the school's commitment to fostering a sense of environmental responsibility among students and has since evolved into a comprehensive program encompassing various aspects of environmental education.

- **Implementation** - The Kothari International School's approach to environmental education involves a multifaceted strategy. The school has established an Environmental Club that includes students from various grades, who participate in activities such as tree planting, waste management, and conservation projects. The curriculum incorporates environmental themes across subjects, encouraging students to explore topics like climate change, biodiversity, and sustainable development through project-based learning and hands-on activities. The school also practices what it preaches by implementing green infrastructure within its campus. This includes rainwater harvesting systems, solar panels, and energy-efficient lighting. Students are involved in the maintenance and monitoring of these systems, providing them with practical knowledge about sustainable technologies. The school has also integrated organic gardening into its curriculum, where students learn about and practice sustainable agriculture techniques.

- **Outcomes** The Green School initiative at Kothari International School has led to significant achievements in both environmental practices and student engagement. The school has successfully reduced its carbon footprint by implementing energy-saving measures and waste management practices. For example, the installation of solar panels has reduced the school's reliance on non-renewable energy sources, while the rainwater harvesting system has improved water conservation efforts. Student participation in environmental activities has increased awareness and action among the school community. The Environmental Club has organized various events such as "Green Fairs" and "Eco-Competitions," which have not only educated students but also involved their families and the local community. Additionally, students have demonstrated improved academic performance and a heightened sense of responsibility towards environmental issues.

- **Impact** The Kothari International School's Green School initiative has had a profound impact on its students, staff, and the surrounding community. By integrating environmental education into both the curriculum and campus operations, the school has created a holistic learning environment that promotes sustainability. The initiative has also inspired other schools in India to adopt similar practices, contributing to a broader movement towards environmental awareness and action in education. The school's success highlights the effectiveness of combining practical sustainability measures with educational programs to foster a culture of environmental stewardship among young learners.

References

Ministry of Environment, Forest and Climate Change, Government of India. "The Environment (Protection) Act, 1986." Retrieved from [India Code](https://www.indiacode.nic.in/handle/123456789/1565?locale=en).

Central Pollution Control Board (CPCB). "The Water (Prevention and Control of Pollution) Act, 1974." Retrieved from [CPCB website](https://cpcb.nic.in/water-pollution/).

Central Pollution Control Board (CPCB). "The Air (Prevention and Control of Pollution) Act, 1981." Retrieved from [CPCB website](https://cpcb.nic.in/air-pollution/).

Ministry of Environment, Forest and Climate Change, Government of India. "The Forest (Conservation) Act, 1980." Retrieved from [India Code](https://www.indiacode.nic.in/handle/123456789/1545?locale=en).

Ministry of Environment, Forest and Climate Change, Government of India. "The Wildlife (Protection) Act, 1972." Retrieved from [India Code](https://www.indiacode.nic.in/handle/123456789/1574?locale=en).

National Green Tribunal (NGT). "The National Green Tribunal Act, 2010." Retrieved from [NGT website](http://greentribunal.gov.in/act).

United Nations Educational, Scientific and Cultural Organization (UNESCO). "Environmental Education." Retrieved from [UNESCO website](https://en.unesco.org/themes/education-sustainable-development/environmental-education).

United States Environmental Protection Agency (EPA). "Environmental Education." Retrieved from [EPA website](https://www.epa.gov/education).

Environmental Protection Agency (EPA) Victoria. "Environmental Education." Retrieved from [EPA Victoria website](https://www.epa.vic.gov.au/about-epa/what-we-do/environmental-education).

The Environment (Protection) Act, 1986.

The Water (Prevention and Control of Pollution) Act, 1974.

The Air (Prevention and Control of Pollution) Act, 1981.

The Forest (Conservation) Act, 1980.

The Wildlife (Protection) Act, 1972.

The National Green Tribunal Act, 2010.

Government of India. (1986). The Environment (Protection) Act. Retrieved from [Ministry of Environment, Forest and Climate Change](http://moef.gov.in/environment-protection-act/).

Government of India. (1974). The Water (Prevention and Control of Pollution) Act. Retrieved from [Central Pollution Control Board](https://cpcb.nic.in/water-pollution-act/).

Government of India. (1981). The Air (Prevention and Control of Pollution) Act. Retrieved from [Central Pollution Control Board](https://cpcb.nic.in/air-pollution-act/).

Government of India. (1980). The Forest (Conservation) Act. Retrieved from [Ministry of Environment, Forest and Climate Change](http://moef.gov.in/forest-conservation-act/).

Government of India. (1972). The Wildlife (Protection) Act. Retrieved from [Ministry of Environment, Forest and Climate Change](http://moef.gov.in/wildlife-protection-act/).

Government of India. (2010). The National Green Tribunal Act. Retrieved from [National Green Tribunal](http://www.greentribunal.gov.in/).

United Nations. (n.d.). Why the Environment Needs Your Help. Retrieved from [United Nations Environment Programme](http://www.unep.org/).

Environmental Protection Agency. (n.d.). Reduce, Reuse, Recycle. Retrieved from [EPA](https://www.epa.gov/recycle).

U.S. Department of Energy. (n.d.). Energy Saver Guide. Retrieved from [Energy.gov](https://www.energy.gov/energysaver/energy-saver-guide).

World Wildlife Fund. (n.d.). How You Can Help. Retrieved from [WWF](https://www.worldwildlife.org/initiatives).

Intergovernmental Panel on Climate Change (IPCC). "Climate Change 2021: The Physical Science Basis." Available at: [IPCC Report](https://www.ipcc.ch/report/ar6/wg1/)

- National Aeronautics and Space Administration (NASA). "Global Climate Change: Evidence." Available at: [NASA Climate](https://climate.nasa.gov/evidence/)

United States Environmental Protection Agency (EPA). "Overview of Greenhouse Gases." Available at: [EPA Greenhouse Gases](https://www.epa.gov/ghgemissions/overview-greenhouse-gases)

- IPCC. "Climate Change 2014: Mitigation of Climate Change." Available at: [IPCC AR5](https://www.ipcc.ch/report/ar5/wg3/)

Food and Agriculture Organization (FAO) of the United Nations. "Global Forest Resources Assessment 2020." Available at: [FAO Forest Assessment](https://www.fao.org/forest-resources-assessment/en/)
- World Wildlife Fund (WWF). "Deforestation and Forest Degradation." Available at: [WWF Deforestation](https://www.worldwildlife.org/threats/deforestation-and-forest-degradation)

International Energy Agency (IEA). "Energy Technology Perspectives 2020." Available at: [IEA Technology Report](https://www.iea.org/reports/energy-technology-perspectives-2020)
- United Nations Environment Programme (UNEP). "Emissions Gap Report 2020." Available at: [UNEP Emissions Gap](https://www.unep.org/emissions-gap-report-2020)

"Climate Change and Land: An IPCC Special Report on Climate Change, Desertification, Land Degradation, Sustainable Land Management, Food Security, and Greenhouse Gas Fluxes in Terrestrial Ecosystems." Available at: [IPCC Land Report](https://www.ipcc.ch/srccl/)

United Nations Human Settlements Programme (UN-Habitat). "World Cities Report 2020." Available at: [UN-Habitat Cities Report](https://unhabitat.org/wcr/)
- IPCC. "Climate Change 2014: Impacts, Adaptation, and Vulnerability." Available at: [IPCC AR5 WG2](https://www.ipcc.ch/report/ar5/wg2/)

National Oceanic and Atmospheric Administration (NOAA). "Climate Change: Global Sea Level." Available at: [NOAA Sea Level](https://www.climate.gov/news-features/understanding-climate/climate-change-global-sea-level)

United Nations Environment Programme (UNEP). "Adaptation Gap Report 2020." Available at: [UNEP Adaptation Gap](https://www.unep.org/adaptation-gap-report-2020)

World Health Organization (WHO). "Climate Change and Health." Available at: [WHO Climate Health](https://www.who.int/health-topics/climate-change#tab=tab_1)

Centers for Disease Control and Prevention (CDC). "Climate Effects on Health." Available at: [CDC Climate Health](https://www.cdc.gov/climateandhealth/effects/default.htm)

The World Bank. "Climate Change: Overview." Available at: [World Bank Climate Overview](https://www.worldbank.org/en/topic/climatechange/overview)

-IPCC. "Climate Change 2014: Impacts, Adaptation, and Vulnerability." Available at: [IPCC AR5 WG2](https://www.ipcc.ch/report/ar5/wg2/)

United Nations Framework Convention on Climate Change (UNFCCC). "Climate Change: Impacts, Vulnerabilities and Adaptation in Developing Countries." Available at: [UNFCCC Impacts](https://unfccc.int/topics/adaptation-and-resilience/the-big-picture/climate-change-impacts-vulnerabilities-and-adaptation-in-developing-countries)

-IPCC. "Climate Change 2014: Impacts, Adaptation, and Vulnerability." Available at: [IPCC AR5 WG2](https://www.ipcc.ch/report/ar5/wg2/)

United Nations Framework Convention on Climate Change (UNFCCC). "The Paris Agreement." Available at: [UNFCCC Paris Agreement](https://unfccc.int/process-

and-meetings/the-paris-agreement/the-paris-agreement)
IPCC. "Climate Change 2021: The Physical Science Basis." Available at: [IPCC AR6 WG1](https://www.ipcc.ch/report/ar6/wg1/)

IPCC. "Climate Change 2014: Mitigation of Climate Change." Available at: [IPCC AR5 WG3](https://www.ipcc.ch/report/ar5/wg3/)
UNEP. "Adaptation Gap Report 2020." Available at: [UNEP Adaptation Gap](https://www.unep.org/adaptation-gap-report-2020)

Millennium Ecosystem Assessment. (2005). Ecosystems and Human Well-being: Synthesis. Island Press.
Convention on Biological Diversity. (2020). Global Biodiversity Outlook 5. Secretariat of the Convention on Biological Diversity.
Chapin III, F. Stuart, et al. (2011). Principles of Terrestrial Ecosystem Ecology. Springer Science & Business Media.
United Nations Environment Programme (UNEP). (2019). Global Environment Outlook – GEO-6: Healthy Planet, Healthy People. Cambridge University Press.
Costanza, Robert, et al. (1997). "The value of the world's ecosystem services and natural capital." Nature 387.6630: 253-260.

Environment (Protection) Act, 1986- Source: Government of India, Ministry of Environment, Forest and Climate Change.

The Water (Prevention and Control of Pollution) Act, 1974 -Source: Government of India, Central Pollution Control Board.

The Air (Prevention and Control of Pollution) Act, 1981 - Government of India, Central Pollution Control Board.

The Forest (Conservation) Act, 1980 - Source: Government of India, Ministry of Environment, Forest and Climate Change.

The Wildlife (Protection) Act, 1972 - Source: Government of India, Ministry of Environment, Forest and Climate Change.

The National Green Tribunal Act, 2010 - Source: Government of India, National Green Tribunal.

The Clean Air Act (CAA) - Source: United States Environmental Protection Agency (EPA).

The Paris Agreement - Source: United Nations Framework Convention on Climate Change (UNFCCC).

The European Green Deal- Source: European Commission.

The Environment (Protection) Act, 1986: Government of India. (1986). The Environment (Protection) Act, 1986. Available from the Ministry of Environment, Forest and Climate Change.

The Water (Prevention and Control of Pollution) Act, 1974: Government of India. (1974). The Water (Prevention and Control of Pollution) Act, 1974. Central Pollution Control Board (CPCB).

The Air (Prevention and Control of Pollution) Act, 1981: Government of India. (1981). The Air (Prevention and Control of Pollution) Act, 1981. Central Pollution Control Board (CPCB).

The Forest (Conservation) Act, 1980: Government of India. (1980). The Forest (Conservation) Act, 1980. Ministry of Environment, Forest and Climate Change.

The Wildlife (Protection) Act, 1972: Government of India. (1972). The Wildlife (Protection) Act, 1972. Wildlife Institute of India.

The National Green Tribunal Act, 2010: Government of

India. (2010). The National Green Tribunal Act, 2010. National Green Tribunal.

Cunningham, W. P., & Cunningham, M. A. (2017). Environmental Science: A Global Concern. McGraw-Hill Education.

Miller, G. T., & Spoolman, S. (2018). Living in the Environment. Cengage Learning.

Carson, R. (2002). Silent Spring. Mariner Books.

Orr, D. W. (1992). Ecological Literacy: Education and the Transition to a Postmodern World. SUNY Press.

United Nations Educational, Scientific and Cultural Organization (UNESCO). (2014). UNESCO Roadmap for Implementing the Global Action Programme on Education for Sustainable Development.

About Author

Other books by Author - (Available online)

- *The Power of Portrayal - Culture & Movies*
- *Consent - The Fundamental Concept*
- *Myths & Misconceptions*
- *Knock Up Parable (Poetries)*
- *Ink & Echoes (Poetries)*

Ashish Shekhar -
BAMMC Faculty, Author, Content Writer & Filmmaker
For any feedback or suggestions write at
ashishshekhar82@gmail.com

Film Suggestions

Films focusing on environmental education

Kadvi Hawa (2017) - A poignant tale addressing the harsh realities of climate change and its impact on rural India, highlighting the struggles of a drought-hit farmer. Director: Nila Madhab Panda. Cast: Sanjay Mishra, Ranvir Shorey, Tillotama Shome

An Inconvenient Truth (2006) - A groundbreaking documentary featuring Al Gore, focusing on the global climate crisis and the urgent need for action. Director: Davis Guggenheim. Cast: Al Gore

Before the Rains (2007) - Set in 1930s Kerala, it tells the story of a British planter whose affair with a local woman threatens to destroy their lives amid environmental challenges. Director: Santosh Sivan. Cast: Rahul Bose, Nandita Das, Linus Roache

Jal (2013) - This film explores the water crisis in the Rann of Kutch, focusing on a man's efforts to find water for his drought-stricken village. Director: Girish Malik. Cast: Purab Kohli, Tannishtha Chatterjee, Kirti Kulhari

The Day After Tomorrow (2004) - A disaster film depicting the catastrophic consequences of climate change, exploring human survival in extreme conditions. Director: Roland Emmerich. Cast: Dennis Quaid, Jake Gyllenhaal, Emmy Rossum

Peepli Live (2010) - While a satire on the media, this film also delves into the environmental and economic issues Indian farmers face. Directors: Anusha Rizvi, Mahmood Farooqui. Cast: Omkar Das Manikpuri, Raghubir Yadav, Naseeruddin Shah

Erin Brockovich (2000) - Inspired by real events, a legal clerk fights to hold a power company accountable for water contamination affecting a small town. Director: Julia Roberts, Albert Finney, Aaron Eckhart

Princess Mononoke (1997) - An epic tale by Studio Ghibli, where a young warrior encounters the battle between industrialization and nature's guardians. Director: Hayao Miyazaki. Voice Cast: Yōji Matsuda, Yuriko Ishida, Yūko Tanaka

Okja (2017) - A powerful story about a young girl who fights to save her genetically modified pet from a large corporation, highlighting animal rights and environmental exploitation issues. Director: Bong Joon-ho. Cast: Ahn Seo-hyun, Tilda Swinton, Paul Dano

www.ingramcontent.com/pod-product-compliance
Lightning Source LLC
Chambersburg PA
CBHW040739120726
48007CB00008B/137